# SONGS OF A SOURDOUGH

By
Robert W. Service

Original Printing by

T. Fisher Unwin, Ltd.
Adelphi Terrace
London, U.K.
1906

Edited by David Abbey, 2015
The Robert Service Series, Volume II

Original Dedication, 1906

"To

C. M."

Dedication of this edition, 2015

To

F.E.A. and C.A.*

*F.E.A. (Fredrick Ephriam Abraham) my father, astonished me one evening by reciting from memory not only "The Shooting of Dan McGrew" but also "The Cremation of Sam McGee". It was then that I knew not all abilities were passed on from father to son. It was a memorable performance, one that I begged him to repeat but to no avail.

*C.A. (Clara Abbey) my mother, always liked Robert Service's poetry, and beyond this she was always fascinated by stories about The North. In her 70th year, on her own, she went north of the Arctic Circle by air; an excursion in a six-seater that flew out of Toronto, touched down for about an hour so that passengers could stretch, buy a coffee and a souvenir, and then returned. She smiled and even giggled a bit as she told of her "Northern exploration".

© David Abbey
Guelph, Ontario, Canada
2015

*The lonely sunsets flare forlorn*
   *Down valleys dreadly desolate;*
*The lordly mountains soar in scorn,*
   *As still as death, as stern as fate.*

   *The lonely sunsets flame and die;*
      *The giant valleys gulp the night;*
   *The monster mountains scrape the sky,*
      *Where eager stars are diamond-bright.*

*So gaunt against the gibbous moon,*
   *Piercing the silence velvet-piled,*
*A lone wolf howls his ancient rune,*
   *The fell arch-spirit of the Wild.*

   *O outcast land! O leper land!*
      *Let the lone wolf-cry all express –*
   *The hate insensate of thy hand,*
      *Thy heart's abysmal loneliness.*

## CONTENTS

|  | Page |
|---|---|
| The Law of the Yukon | 9 |
| The Parson's Son | 13 |
| The Spell of the Yukon | 17 |
| The Call of the Wild | 23 |
| The Lone Trail | 27 |
| The Heart of the Sourdough | 29 |
| The Three Voices | 31 |
| The Pines | 33 |
| The Harpy | 37 |
| The Lure of Little Voices | 41 |
| The Song of the Wage-Slave | 43 |
| Grin | 47 |
| The Shooting of Dan McGrew | 49 |
| The Cremation of Sam McGee | 55 |
| My Madonna | 61 |
| Unforgotten | 63 |
| The Reckoning | 65 |
| Quatrains | 67 |
| The Men that Don't Fit In | 69 |
| Music in the Bush | 71 |
| The Rhyme of the Remittance Man | 75 |
| The Low-Down White | 79 |
| The Little Log-Cabin | 81 |
| The Younger Son | 83 |
| The March of the Dead | 87 |
| "Fighting Mac" | 91 |
| The Woman and the Angel | 95 |
| The Rhyme of the Restless Ones | 97 |
| New Year's Eve | 101 |
| Comfort | 105 |
| Premonition | 107 |
| The Tramps | 109 |
| L'envoi | 111 |

## THE LAW OF THE YUKON

THIS is the law of the Yukon, and ever she makes it plain:
"Send not your foolish and feeble; send me your strong and your sane.
Strong for the red rage of battle; sane, for I harry them sore;
Send me men girt for the combat, men who are grit to the core;
Swift as the panther in triumph, fierce as the bear in defeat,
Sired of a bulldog parent, steeled in the furnace heat.
Send me the best of your breeding, lend me your chosen ones;
Them will I take to my bosom, them will I call my sons;
Them will I gild with my treasure, them will I glut with my meat;
But the others — the misfits, the failures — I trample under my feet.
Dissolute, damned, and despairful, crippled and palsied and slain,
Ye would send me the spawn of your gutters — Go! take back your spawn
    again.

"Wild and wide are my borders, stern as death is my sway;
From my ruthless throne I have ruled alone for a million years and a day;
Hugging my mighty treasure, waiting for man to come:
Till he swept like a turbid torrent, and after him swept — the scum.
The pallid pimp of the dead-line, the enervate of the pen,
One by one I weeded them out, for all that I sought was — Men.
One by one I dismayed them, frighting them sore with my glooms;
One by one I betrayed them unto my manifold dooms.
Drowned them like rats in my rivers, starved them like curs on my plains,
Rotted the flesh that was left them, poisoned the blood in their veins;
Burst with my winter upon them, searing forever their sight,
Lashed them with fungus-white faces, whimpering wild in the night;
Staggering blind through the storm-whirl, stumbling mad through the
    snow,
Frozen stiff in the ice pack, brittle and bent like a bow;
Featureless, formless, forsaken, scented by wolves in their flight,
Left for the wind to make music through ribs that are glittering white;
Gnawing the black crust of failure, searching the pit of despair,
Crooking the toe in the trigger, trying to patter a prayer;
Going outside with an escort, raving with lips all afoam;
Writing a cheque for a million, drivelling feebly of home;
Lost like a louse in the burning ... or else in tented town
Seeking a drunkard's solace, sinking and sinking down;
Steeped in the slime at the bottom, dead to a decent world,
Lost 'mid the human flotsam, far on the frontier hurled;

In the camp at the bend of the river, with its dozen saloons aglare,
Its gambling dens a-riot, its gramophones all a-blare;
Crimped with the crimes of a city, sin-ridden and bridled with lies,
In the hush of my mountained vastness, in the flush of my midnight skies.
Plague-spots, yet tools of my purpose, so natheless I suffer them thrive,
Crushing my Weak in their clutches, that only my Strong may survive.

"But the others, the men of my mettle, the men who would 'stablish my fame,
Unto its ultimate issue, winning me honour, not shame;
Searching my uttermost valleys, fighting each step as they go,
Shooting the wrath of my rapids, scaling my ramparts of snow;
Ripping the guts of my mountains, looting the beds of my creeks,
Them will I take to my bosom, and speak as a mother speaks.

I am the land that listens, I am the land that broods;
Steeped in eternal beauty, crystalline waters and woods.
Long have I waited lonely, shunned as a thing accurst,
Monstrous, moody, pathetic, the last of the lands and the first;
Visioning camp-fires at twilight, sad with a longing forlorn,
Feeling my womb o'er-pregnant with the seed of cities unborn.
Wild and wide are my borders, stern as death is my sway,
And I wait for the men who will win me — and I will not be won in a day;
And I will not be won by weaklings, subtile, suave, and mild,
But by men with the hearts of vikings, and the simple faith of a child;
Desperate, strong, and resistless, unthrottled by fear or defeat,
Them will I gild with my treasure, them will I glut with my meat.

"Lofty I stand from each sister land, patient and wearily wise,
With the weight of a world of sadness in my quiet, passionless eyes;
Dreaming alone of a people, dreaming alone of a day,
When men shall not rape my riches, and curse me and go away;
Making a bawd of my bounty, fouling the hand that gave —
Till I rise in my wrath and I sweep on their path and I stamp them into a grave.
Dreaming of men who will bless me, of women esteeming me good,
Of children born in my borders, of radiant motherhood;
Of cities leaping to stature, of fame like a flag unfurled,
As I pour the tide of my riches in the eager lap of the world."

This is the Law of the Yukon, that only the Strong shall thrive;
That surely the Weak shall perish, and only the Fit survive.
Dissolute, damned, and despairful, crippled and palsied and slain,
This is the Will of the Yukon, — Lo! how she makes it plain!

## THE PARSON'S SON

*THIS is the song of the parson's son, as he squats in his shack alone,*
*On the wild, weird nights when the Northern Lights shoot up from the frozen zone,*
*And it's sixty below, and couched in the snow the hungry huskies moan.*

"I'm one of the Arctic brotherhood, I'm an old-time pioneer.
I came with the first—O God! how I've cursed this Yukon—but still I'm here.
I've sweated athirst in its summer heat, I've frozen and starved in its cold;
I've followed my dreams by its thousand streams, I've toiled and moiled for its gold.
"Look at my eyes—been snow-blind twice; look where my foot's half gone;
And that gruesome scar on my left cheek where the frost-fiend bit to the bone.
Each one a brand of this devil's land, where I've played and I've lost the game,
A broken wreck with a craze for 'hooch,' and never a cent to my name.

"This mining is only a gamble, the worst is as good as the best;
I was in with the bunch and I might have come out right on top with the rest;
With Cormack, Ladue and Macdonald—O God! but it's hell to think
Of the thousands and thousands I've squandered on cards and women and drink.
"In the early days we were just a few, and we hunted and fished around,
Nor dreamt by our lonely camp-fires of the wealth that lay under the ground.
We traded in skins and whiskey, and I've often slept under the shade
Of that lone birch-tree on Bonanza, where the first big find was made.

"We were just like a great big family, and every man had his squaw,
And we lived such a wild, free, fearless life beyond the pale of the law;

Till sudden there came a whisper, and it maddened us every man,
And I got in on Bonanza before the big rush began.

"Oh, those Dawson days, and the sin and the blaze, and the town all open wide!
(If God made me in His likeness, sure He let the devil inside.)
But we all were mad, both the good and the bad, and as for the women, well—
No spot on the map in so short a space has hustled more souls to hell.

"Money was just like dirt there, easy to get and to spend.
I was all caked in on a dance-hall jade, but she shook me in the end.
It put me queer, and for near a year I never drew sober breath,
Till I found myself in the bughouse ward with a claim staked out on death.

"Twenty years in the Yukon, struggling along its creeks;
Roaming its giant valleys, scaling its god-like peaks;
Bathed in its fiery sunsets, fighting its fiendish cold,
Twenty years in the Yukon ... twenty years—and I'm old.

"Old and weak, but no matter, there's 'hooch' in the bottle still.
I'll hitch up the dogs to-morrow, and mush down the trail to Bill.
It's so long dark, and I'm lonesome—I'll just lay down on the bed,
To-morrow I'll go ... to-morrow ... I guess I'll play on the red.

"... Come, Kit, your pony is saddled. I'm waiting, dear, in the court ...
... Minnie, you devil, I'll kill you if you skip with that flossy sport ...
... How much does it go to the pan, Bill?... play up, School, and play the game
... Our Father, which art in heaven, hallowed be Thy name ..."

This was the song of the parson's son, as he lay in his bunk alone,
Ere the fire went out and the cold crept in, and his blue lips ceased to moan,
And the hunger-maddened malamutes had torn him flesh from bone.

## THE SPELL OF THE YUKON

I WANTED the gold, and I sought it;
    I scrabbled and mucked like a slave.
Was it famine or scurvy—I fought it,
    I hurled my youth into the grave.
I wanted the gold and I got it—
    Came out with a fortune last fall,—
Yet somehow life's not what I thought it,
    And somehow the gold isn't all.

No! There's the land. (Have you seen it?)
    It's the cussedest land that I know,
From the big, dizzy mountains that screen it,
    To the deep, deathlike valleys below.
Some say God was tired when He made it;
    Some say it's a fine land to shun;
Maybe: but there's some as would trade it
    For no land on earth—and I'm one.

You come to get rich (damned good reason),
    You feel like an exile at first;
You hate it like hell for a season,
    And then you are worse than the worst.
It grips you like some kinds of sinning;
    It twists you from foe to a friend;
It seems it's been since the beginning;
    It seems it will be to the end.

I've stood in some mighty-mouthed hollow
    That's plumb-full of hush to the brim;
I've watched the big, husky sun wallow
    In crimson and gold, and grow dim,
Till the moon set the pearly peaks gleaming,
    And the stars tumbled out, neck and crop;
And I've thought that I surely was dreaming,
    With the peace o' the world piled on top.

The summer—no sweeter was ever;
    The sunshiny woods all athrill;
The grayling aleap in the river,
    The bighorn asleep on the hill.
The strong life that never knows harness;
    The wilds where the caribou call;
The freshness, the freedom, the farness—
    O God! how I'm stuck on it all.

The winter! the brightness that blinds you,
    The white land locked tight as a drum,
The cold fear that follows and finds you,
    The silence that bludgeons you dumb.
The snows that are older than history,
    The woods where the weird shadows slant;
The stillness, the moonlight, the mystery,
    I've bade 'em good-bye—but I can't.

There's a land where the mountains are nameless,
    And the rivers all run God knows where;
There are lives that are erring and aimless,
    And deaths that just hang by a hair;
There are hardships that nobody reckons;
    There are valleys unpeopled and still;
There's a land—oh, it beckons and beckons,
    And I want to go back—and I will.

They're making my money diminish;
    I'm sick of the taste of champagne.
Thank God! when I'm skinned to a finish
    I'll pike to the Yukon again.
I'll fight—and you bet it's no sham-fight;
    It's hell!—but I've been there before;
And it's better than this by a damsite—
    So me for the Yukon once more.

There's gold, and it's haunting and haunting;
    It's luring me on as of old;
Yet it isn't the gold that I'm wanting,
    So much as just finding the gold.
It's the great, big, broad land 'way up yonder,
    It's the forests where silence has lease;
It's the beauty that thrills me with wonder,
    It's the stillness that fills me with peace.

## THE CALL OF THE WILD

HAVE you gazed on naked grandeur where there's nothing else to gaze on,
    Set pieces and drop-curtain scenes galore,
Big mountains heaved to heaven, which the blinding sunsets blazon,
    Black canyons where the rapids rip and roar?
Have you swept the visioned valley with the green stream streaking through ,
    Searched the Vastness for a something you have lost?
Have you strung your soul to silence? Then for God's sake go and do it;
    Hear the challenge, learn the lesson, pay the cost.

Have you wandered in the wilderness, the sage-brush desolation,
    The bunch-grass levels where the cattle graze?
Have you whistled bits of rag-time at the end of all creation,
    And learned to know the desert's little ways?
Have you camped upon the foothills, have you galloped o'er the ranges,
    Have you roamed the arid sun-lands through and through?
Have you chummed up with the mesa? Do you know its moods and changes?
    Then listen to the wild—it's calling you.

Have you known the Great White Silence, not a snow-gemmed twig a-quiver?
    (Eternal truths that shame our soothing lies.)
Have you broken trail on snowshoes? mushed your huskies up the river,
    Dared the unknown, led the way, and clutched the prize?
Have you marked the map's void spaces, mingled with the mongrel races,
    Felt the savage strength of brute in every thew?
And though grim as hell the worst is, can you round it off with curses?
    Then hearken to the wild—it's wanting you.

Have you suffered, starved, and triumphed grovelled, down, yet grasped at glory,
    Grown bigger in the bigness of the whole?
"Done things" just for the doing, letting babblers tell the story,
    Seeing through the nice veneer the naked soul?

Have you seen God in His splendours, heard the text that nature renders?
   (You'll never hear it in the family pew.)
The simple things, the true things, the silent men who do things—
   Then listen to the wild—it's calling you.

They have cradled you in custom, they have primed you with their
   preaching,
They have soaked you in convention through and through;
They have put you in a showcase; you're a credit to their teaching—
   But can't you hear the wild?—it's calling you.
Let us probe the silent places, let us seek what luck betide us;
   Let us journey to a lonely land I know.
There's a whisper on the night-wind, there's a star agleam to guide us,
   And the wild is calling, calling ... let us go.

## THE LONE TRAIL

YE who know the Lone Trail fain would follow it,
Though it lead to glory or the darkness of the pit.
Ye who take the Lone Trail, bid your love good-bye;
The Lone Trail, the Lone Trail follow till you die.

The trails of the world be countless, and most of the trails be tried;
You tread on the heels of the many, till you come where the ways divide;
And one lies safe in the sunlight, and the other is dreary and wan,
Yet you look aslant at the Lone Trail, and the Lone Trail lures you on.
And somehow you're sick of the highway, with its noise and its easy needs,
And you seek the risk of the by-way, and you reck not where it leads.
And sometimes it leads to the desert, and the tongue swells out of the mouth,
And you stagger blind to the mirage, to die in the mocking drouth.
And sometimes it leads to the mountain, to the light of the lone camp-fire,
And you gnaw your belt in the anguish of hunger-goaded desire.
And sometimes it leads to the Southland, to the swamp where the orchid glows,
And you rave to your grave with the fever, and they rob the corpse for its clothes.
And sometimes it leads to the Northland, and the scurvy softens your bones,
And your flesh dints in like putty, and you spit out your teeth like stones.
And sometimes it leads to a coral reef in the wash of a weedy sea,
And you sit and stare at the empty glare where the gulls wait greedily.
And sometimes it leads to an Arctic trail, and the snows where your torn feet freeze,
And you whittle away the useless clay, and crawl on your hands and knees.
Often it leads to the dead-pit; always it leads to pain;
By the bones of your brothers ye know it, but oh, to follow you're fain.
By your bones they will follow behind you, till the ways of the world are made plain.
Bid good-bye to sweetheart, bid good-bye to friend;
The Lone Trail, the Lone Trail follow to the end.
Tarry not, and fear not, chosen of the true;
Lover of the Lone Trail, the Lone Trail waits for you.

## THE HEART OF THE SOURDOUGH

THERE where the mighty mountains bare their fangs unto the moon;
There where the sullen sun-dogs glare in the snow-bright, bitter noon,
And the glacier-gutted streams sweep down at the clarion call of June:

There where the livid tundras keep their tryst with the tranquil snows;
There where the Silences are spawned, and the light of hell-fire flows
Into the bowl of the midnight sky, violet, amber, and rose:

There where the rapids churn and roar, and the ice-floes bellowing run;
Where the tortured, twisted rivers of blood rush to the setting sun—
I've packed my kit and I'm going, boys, ere another day is done.

I knew it would call, or soon or late, as it calls the whirring wings;
It's the olden lure, it's the golden lure, it's the lure of the timeless things;
And to-night, O God of the trails untrod, how it whines in my heart-strings!

I'm sick to death of your well-groomed gods, your make-believe and your show;
I long for a whiff of bacon and beans, a snug shake-down in the snow,
A trail to break, and a life at stake, and another bout with the foe;

With the raw-ribbed Wild that abhors all life, the wild that would crush and rend;
I have clinched and closed with the naked North, I have learned to defy and defend;
Shoulder to shoulder we've fought it out—yet the Wild must win in the end.

I have flouted the Wild. I have followed its lure, fearless, familiar, alone;
By all that the battle means and makes I claim that land for mine own;
Yet the Wild must win, and a day will come when I shall be overthrown.

Then when as wolf-dogs fight we've fought, the lean wolf-land and I;
Fought and bled till the snows are red under the reeling sky;
Even as lean wolf-dog goes down will I go down and die.

## THE THREE VOICES

THE waves have a story to tell me,
    As I lie on the lonely beach;
Chanting aloft in the pine-tops,
    The wind has a lesson to teach;
But the stars sing an anthem of glory
    I cannot put into speech.

The waves tell of ocean spaces,
    Of hearts that are wild and brave,
Of populous city places,
    Of desolate shores they lave;
Of men who sally in quest of gold
    To sink in an ocean grave.

The wind is a mighty roamer;
    He bids me keep me free,
Clean from the taint of the gold-lust,
    Hardy and pure as he;
Cling with my love to nature
    As a child to the mother-knee.

But the stars throng out in their glory,
    And they sing of the God in man;
They sing of the mighty Master,
    Of the loom His fingers span;
Where a star or a soul is a part of the whole,
    And weft in the wondrous plan.

Here by the camp-fire's flicker,
    Deep in my blanket curled,
I long for the peace of the pine-gloom
    When the scroll of the Lord is unfurled,
And the wind and the wave are silent,
    And world is singing to world.

## THE PINES

WE sleep in the sleep of ages, the bleak, barbarian pines;
The grey moss drapes us like sages, and closer we lock our lines,
And deeper we clutch through the gelid gloom where never a sunbeam shines.

On the flanks of the storm-gored ridges are our black battalions massed;
We surge in a host to the sullen coast, and we sing in the ocean blast;
From empire of sea to empire of snow we grip our empire fast.

To the niggard lands were we driven; 'twixt desert and foe are we penned.
To us was the Northland given, ours to stronghold and defend;
Ours till the world be riven in the crash of the utter end.

Ours from the bleak beginning, through the æons of death-like sleep;
Ours from the shock when the naked rock was hurled from the hissing deep;
Ours through the twilight ages of weary glacier-creep.

Wind of the East, wind of the West, wandering to and fro,
Chant your songs in our topmost boughs, that the sons of men may know
The peerless pine was the first to come, and the pine will be last to go!

We pillar the halls of perfumed gloom; we plume where the eagles soar;
The North-wind swoops from the brooding Pole, our ancients crash and roar;
But where one falls from the crumbling walls shoots up a hardy score.

We spring from the gloom of the canyon's womb; in the valley's lap we lie;
From the white foam-fringe where the breakers cringe to the peaks that tusk the sky
We climb, and we peer in the crag-locked mere that gleams like a golden eye,—

Gain to the verge of the hog-back ridge where the vision ranges free:
Pines and pines and the shadow of pines as far as the eye can see;
A steadfast legion of stalwart knights in dominant empery.

Sun, moon and stars, give answer; shall we not staunchly stand
Even as now, forever, wards of the wilder strand,
Sentinels of the stillness, lords of the last lone land!

## THE HARPY

THERE was a woman, and she was wise; woefully wise was she;
She was old, so old, yet her years all told were but a score and three;
And she knew by heart, from finish to start, the Book of Iniquity.

There is no hope for such as I, on earth nor yet in Heaven;
Unloved I live, unloved I die, unpitied, unforgiven;
A loathèd jade I ply my trade, unhallowed and unshriven.

I paint my cheeks, for they are white, and cheeks of chalk men hate;
Mine eyes with wine I make to shine, that men may seek and sate;
With overhead a lamp of red I sit me down and wait.

Until they come, the nightly scum, with drunken eyes aflame;
Your sweethearts, sons, ye scornful ones—'tis I who know their shame;
The gods ye see are brutes to me—and so I play my game.

For life is not the thing we thought, and not the thing we plan;
And woman in a bitter world must do the best she can;
Must yield the stroke, and bear the yoke, and serve the will of man;

Must serve his need and ever feed the flame of his desire;
Though be she loved for love alone, or be she loved for hire;
For every man since life began is tainted with the mire.

And though you know he love you so, and set you on love's throne,
Yet let your eyes but mock his sighs, and let your heart be stone,
Lest you be left (as I was left) attainted and alone.

From love's close kiss to hell's abyss is one sheer flight, I trow;
And wedding-ring and bridal bell are will-o'-wisps of woe;
And 'tis not wise to love too well, and this all women know.

Wherefore, the wolf-pack having gorged upon the lamb, their prey,
With siren smile and serpent guile I make the wolf-pack pay;
With velvet paws and flensing claws, a tigress roused to slay.

One who in youth sought truest truth, and found a devil's lies;
A symbol of the sin of man, a human sacrifice:
Yet shall I blame on man the shame? Could it be otherwise?

Was I not born to walk in scorn where others walk in pride?
The Maker marred, and evil-starred I drift upon His tide;
And He alone shall judge His own, so I His judgment bide.

Fate has written a tragedy; its name is "The Human Heart."
The theatre is the House of Life, Woman the mummer's part:
The Devil enters the prompter's box and the play is ready to start.

## THE LURE OF LITTLE VOICES

THERE'S a cry from out the Loneliness—Oh, listen, Honey, listen!
    Do you hear it, do you fear it, you're a-holding of me so?
You're a-sobbing in your sleep, dear, and your lashes, how they glisten—
    Do you hear the Little Voices all a-begging me to go?

All a-begging me to leave you. Day and night they're pleading, praying,
    On the North-wind, on the West-wind, from the peak and from the plain;
Night and day they never leave me—do you know what they are saying?
    "He was ours before you got him, and we want him once again."

Yes, they're wanting me, they're haunting me, the awful lonely places;
    They're whining and they're whimpering as if each had a soul;
They're calling from the wilderness, the vast and god-like spaces,
    The stark and sullen solitudes that sentinel the Pole.

They miss my little camp-fires, ever brightly, bravely gleaming
    In the womb of desolation where was never man before;
As comradeless I sought them, lion-hearted, loving, dreaming;
    And they hailed me as a comrade, and they loved me evermore.

And now they're all a-crying, and it's no use me denying:
    The spell of them is on me and I'm helpless as a child;
My heart is aching, aching, but I hear them sleeping, waking;
    It's the Lure of Little Voices, it's the mandate of the Wild.

I'm afraid to tell you, Honey, I can take no bitter leaving;
    But softly in the sleep-time from your love I'll steal away.
Oh, it's cruel, dearie, cruel, and it's God knows how I'm grieving;
    But His Loneliness is calling and He knows I must obey.

## THE SONG OF THE WAGE-SLAVE

WHEN the long, long day is over, and the Big Boss gives me my pay,
I hope that it won't be hell-fire, as some of the parsons say.
And I hope that it won't be heaven, with some of the parsons I've met—
All I want is just quiet, just to rest and forget.
Look at my face, toil-furrowed; look at my calloused hands;
Master, I've done Thy bidding, wrought in Thy many lands—
Wrought for the little masters, big-bellied they be, and rich;
I've done their desire for a daily hire, and I die like a dog in a ditch.
I have used the strength Thou hast given, Thou knowest I did not shirk;
Threescore years of labour—Thine be the long day's work.
And now, Big Master, I'm broken and bent and twisted and scarred,
But I've held my job, and Thou knowest, and Thou wilt not judge me hard.
Thou knowest my sins are many, and often I've played the fool—
Whiskey and cards and women, they made me the devil's tool.
I was just like a child with money: I flung it away with a curse,
Feasting a fawning parasite, or glutting a harlot's purse,
Then back to the woods repentant, back to the mill or the mine,
I, the worker of workers, everything in my line.
Everything hard but headwork (I'd no more brains than a kid),
A brute with brute strength to labour, doing as I was bid;
Living in camps with men-folk, a lonely and loveless life;
Never knew kiss of sweetheart, never caress of wife.
A brute with brute strength to labour, and they were so far above—
Yet I'd gladly have gone to the gallows for one little look of Love.
I with the strength of two men, savage and shy and wild—
Yet how I'd ha' treasured a woman, and the sweet, warm kiss of a child.
Well, 'tis Thy world, and Thou knowest. I blaspheme and my ways be rude;
But I've lived my life as I found it, and I've done my best to be good;
I, the primitive toiler, half naked, and grimed to the eyes,
Sweating it deep in their ditches, swining it stark in their styes
Hulling down forests before me, spanning tumultuous streams;
Down in the ditch building o'er me palaces fairer than dreams;
Boring the rock to the ore-bed, driving the road through the fen,

Resolute, dumb, uncomplaining, a man in a world of men.
Master, I've filled my contract, wrought in Thy many lands;
Not by my sins wilt Thou judge me, but by the work of my hands.
Master, I've done Thy bidding, and the light is low in the west,
And the long, long shift is over ... Master, I've earned it—Rest.

## GRIN

IF you're up against a bruiser and you're getting knocked about—
        Grin.
If you're feeling pretty groggy, and you're licked beyond a doubt—
        Grin.
Don't let him see you're funking, let him know with every clout,
Though your face is battered to a pulp, your blooming heart is stout;
Just stand upon your pins until the beggar knocks you out—
        And grin.
This life's a bally battle, and the same advice holds true,
        Of grin.
If you're up against it badly, then it's only one on you,
        So grin.
If the future's black as thunder, don't let people see you're blue;
Just cultivate a cast-iron smile of joy the whole day through;
If they call you "Little Sunshine," wish that they'd no troubles, too—
        You may—grin.
Rise up in the morning with the will that, smooth or rough,
        You'll grin.
Sink to sleep at midnight, and although you're feeling tough,
        Yet grin.
There's nothing gained by whining, and you're not that kind of stuff;
You're a fighter from away back, and you won't take a rebuff;
Your trouble is that you don't know when you have had enough—
        Don't give in.
If Fate should down you, just get up and take another cuff;
You may bank on it that there is no philosophy like bluff
        And grin.

]

## THE SHOOTING OF DAN MCGREW

A BUNCH of the boys were whooping it up in the Malamute saloon;
The kid that handles the music-box was hitting a jag-time tune;
Back of the bar, in a solo game, sat Dangerous Dan McGrew,
And watching his luck was his light-o'-love, the lady that's known as Lou.

When out of the night, which was fifty below, and into the din and the glare,
There stumbled a miner fresh from the creeks, dog-dirty and loaded for bear.
He looked like a man with a foot in the grave, and scarcely the strength of a louse,
Yet he tilted a poke of dust on the bar, and he called for drinks for the house.
There was none could place the stranger's face, though we searched ourselves for a clue;
But we drank his health, and the last to drink was Dangerous Dan McGrew.

There's men that somehow just grip your eyes, and hold them hard like a spell;
And such was he, and he looked to me like a man who had lived in hell;
With a face most hair, and the dreary stare of a dog whose day is done,
As he watered the green stuff in his glass, and the drops fell one by one.
Then I got to figgering who he was, and wondering what he'd do,
And I turned my head—and there watching him was the lady that's known as Lou.

His eyes went rubbering round the room, and he seemed in a kind of daze,
Till at last that old piano fell in the way of his wandering gaze.
The rag-time kid was having a drink; there was no one else on the stool,
So the stranger stumbles across the room, and flops down there like a fool.
In a buckskin shirt that was glazed with dirt he sat, and I saw him sway;
Then he clutched the keys with his talon hands—my God! but that man could   play!

Were you ever out in the Great Alone, when the moon was awful clear,
And the icy mountains hemmed you in with a silence you most could hear;
With only the howl of a timber wolf, and you camped there in the cold,

A half-dead thing in a stark, dead world, clean mad for the muck called
    gold;
While high overhead, green, yellow, and red, the North Lights swept in
    bars—
Then you've a haunch what the music meant ... hunger and night and the
    stars.

And hunger not of the belly kind, that's banished with bacon and beans;
But the gnawing hunger of lonely men for a home and all that it means;
For a fireside far from the cares that are, four walls and a roof above;
But oh! so cramful of cosy joy, and crowned with a woman's love;
A woman dearer than all the world, and true as Heaven is true—
(God! how ghastly she looks through her rouge,—the lady that's known as
    Lou.)

Then on a sudden the music changed, so soft that you scarce could hear;
But you felt that your life had been looted clean of all that it once held
    dear;
That someone had stolen the woman you loved; that her love was a devil's
    lie;
That your guts were gone, and the best for you was to crawl away and die.
'Twas the crowning cry of a heart's despair, and it thrilled you through and
    through—
"I guess I'll make it a spread misere," said Dangerous Dan McGrew.

The music almost died away ... then it burst like a pent-up flood;
And it seemed to say, "Repay, repay," and my eyes were blind with blood.
The thought came back of an ancient wrong, and it stung like a frozen lash,
And the lust awoke to kill, to kill ... then the music stopped with a crash,

And the stranger turned, and his eyes they burned in a most peculiar way;
In a buckskin shirt that was glazed with dirt he sat, and I saw him sway;
Then his lips went in in a kind of grin, and he spoke, and his voice was
    calm;
And, "Boys," says he, "you don't know me, and none of you care a damn;

But I want to state, and my words are straight, and I'll bet my poke they're
    true,
That one of you is a hound of hell ... and that one is Dan McGrew."

Then I ducked my head, and the lights went out, and two guns blazed in the dark;
And a woman screamed, and the lights went up, and two men lay stiff and stark;
Pitched on his head, and pumped full of lead, was Dangerous Dan McGrew,
While the man from the creeks lay clutched to the breast of the lady that's known as Lou.

These are the simple facts of the case, and I guess I ought to know;
They say that the stranger was crazed with "hooch," and I'm not denying it's so.
I'm not so wise as the lawyer guys, but strictly between us two—
The woman that kissed him and—pinched his poke—was the lady that's known as Lou.

## THE CREMATION OF SAM MCGEE

THERE are strange things done in the midnight sun
    By the men who moil for gold;
The Arctic trails have their secret tales
    That would make your blood run cold;
The Northern Lights have seen queer sights,
    But the queerest they ever did see
Was that night on the marge of Lake Lebarge
    I cremated Sam McGee.

Now Sam McGee was from Tennessee, where the cotton blooms and blows.
Why he left his home in the South to roam round the Pole God only knows.
He was always cold, but the land of gold seemed to hold him like a spell;
Though he'd often say in his homely way that he'd "sooner live in hell."

On a Christmas Day we were mushing our way over the Dawson trail.
Talk of your cold! through the parka's fold it stabbed like a driven nail.
If our eyes we'd close, then the lashes froze, till sometimes we couldn't see;
It wasn't much fun, but the only one to whimper was Sam McGee.

And that very night as we lay packed tight in our robes beneath the snow,
And the dogs were fed, and the stars o'erhead were dancing heel and toe,
He turned to me, and, "Cap," says he, "I'll cash in this trip, I guess;
And if I do, I'm asking that you won't refuse my last request."

Well, he seemed so low that I couldn't say no: then he says with a sort of moan:
"It's the cursèd cold, and it's got right hold till I'm chilled clean through to the bone.
Yet 'taint being dead, it's my awful dread of the icy grave that pains:
So I want you to swear that, foul or fair, you'll cremate my last remains."

A pal's last need is a thing to heed, so I swore I would not fail;
And we started on at the streak of dawn, but God! he looked ghastly pale.
He crouched on the sleigh, and he raved all day of his home in Tennessee;
And before nightfall a corpse was all that was left of Sam McGee.

There wasn't a breath in that land of death, and I hurried, horror driven,
With a corpse half-hid that I couldn't get rid because of a promise given;
It was lashed to the sleigh, and it seemed to say: "You may tax your brawn and brains,
But you promised true, and it's up to you to cremate those last remains."

Now a promise made is a debt unpaid, and the trail has its own stern code.
In the days to come, though my lips were dumb, in my heart how I cursed that load.
In the long, long night, by the lone firelight, while the huskies, round in a ring,
Howled out their woes to the homeless snows—O God! how I loathed the thing!

And every day that quiet clay seemed to heavy and heavier grow;
And on I went, though the dogs were spent and the grub was getting low;
The trail was bad, and I felt half mad, but I swore I would not give in;
And I'd often sing to the hateful thing, and it hearkened with a grin.

Till I came to the marge of Lake Lebarge, and a derelict there lay;
It was jammed in the ice, but I saw in a trice it was called the "Alice May."
And I looked at it, and I thought a bit, and I looked at my frozen chum:
Then, "Here," said I, with a sudden cry, "is my cre-ma-tor-eum."

Some planks I tore from the cabin floor, and I lit the boiler fire;
Some coal I found that was lying around, and I heaped the fuel higher;
The flames just soared, and the furnace roared—such a blaze you seldom see;
And I burrowed a hole in the glowing coal, and I stuffed in Sam McGee.

Then I made a hike, for I didn't like to hear him sizzle so;
And the heavens scowled, and the huskies howled, and the wind began to blow.
It was icy cold, but the hot sweat rolled down my cheeks, and I don't know why;
And the greasy smoke in an inky cloak went streaking down the sky.

I do not know how long in the snow I wrestled with grisly fear;
But the stars came out and they danced about ere again I ventured near;
I was sick with dread, but I bravely said: "I'll just take a peep inside.

 I guess he's cooked, and it's time I looked," ... then the door I opened wide.

And there sat Sam, looking cool and calm, in the heart of the furnace roar;
And he wore a smile you could see a mile, and he said: "Please close that door.
It's fine in here, but I greatly fear you'll let in the cold and storm—
Since I left Plumtree, down in Tennessee, it's the first time I've been warm."

There are strange things done in the midnight sun
    By the men who moil for gold;
The Arctic trails have their secret tales
    That would make your blood run cold;
The Northern Lights have seen queer sights,
    But the queerest they ever did see
Was that night on the marge of Lake Lebarge
    I cremated Sam McGee.

## MY MADONNA

I HALED me a woman from the street,
   Shameless, but, oh, so fair!
I bade her sit in the model's seat,
   And I painted her sitting there.

   I hid all trace of her heart unclean;
      I painted a babe at her breast;
   I painted her as she might have been
      If the Worst had been the Best.

She laughed at my picture, and went away.
   Then came, with a knowing nod,
A connoisseur, and I heard him say:
   "'Tis Mary, the Mother of God."

   So I painted a halo round her hair,
      And I sold her, and took my fee,
   And she hangs in the church of Saint Hilaire,
      Where you and all may see.

## UNFORGOTTEN

I KNOW a garden where the lilies gleam,
   And one who lingers in the sunshine there;
   She is than white-stoled lily far more fair,
And oh, her eyes are heaven-lit with dream.

   I know a garret, cold and dark and drear,
      And one who toils and toils with tireless pen,
      Until his brave, sad eyes grow weary—then
   He seeks the stars, pale, silent as a seer.

And ah, it's strange, for desolate and dim
   Between these two there rolls an ocean wide;
   Yet he is in the garden by her side,
And she is in the garret there with him.

## THE RECKONING

IT'S fine to have a blow-out in a fancy restaurant,
With terrapin and canvas-back and all the wine you want;
To enjoy the flowers and music, watch the pretty women pass,
Smoke a choice cigar, and sip the wealthy water in your glass;
It's bully in a high-toned joint to eat and drink your fill,
But it's quite another matter when you
      Pay the bill.

It's great to go out every night on fun or pleasure bent,
To wear your glad rags always, and to never save a cent;
To drift along regardless, have a good time every trip;
To hit the high spots sometimes, and to let your chances slip;
To know you're acting foolish, yet to go on fooling still,
Till Nature calls a show-down, and you
      Pay the bill.

 Time has got a little bill—get wise while yet you may,
For the debit side's increasing in a most alarming way;
The things you had no right to do, the things you should have done,
They're all put down: it's up to you to pay for every one.
  So eat, drink, and be merry, have a good time if you will,
  But God help you when the time comes, and you
      Foot the bill.

## QUATRAINS

ONE said: Thy life is thine to make or mar,
To flicker feebly, or to soar, a star;
It lies with thee—the choice is thine, is thine,
To hit the ties or drive thy auto-car.

I answer Her: The choice is mine—ah, no!
We all were made or marred long, long ago.
The parts are written: hear the super wail:
"Who is stage-managing this cosmic show?"

Blind fools of fate, and slaves of circumstance,
Life is a fiddler, and we all must dance.
From gloom where mocks that will-o'-wisp, Freewill,
I heard a voice cry: "Say, give us a chance."

Chance! Oh, there is no chance. The scene is set.
Up with the curtain! Man, the marionette,
Resumes his part. The gods will work the wires.
They've got it all down fine, you bet, you bet!

It's all decreed: the mighty earthquake crash;
The countless constellations' wheel and flash;
The rise and fall of empires, war's red tide,
The composition of your dinner hash.

There's no haphazard in this world of ours:
Cause and effect are grim, relentless powers.
They rule the world. (A king was shot last night.
Last night I held the joker and both bowers.)

From out the mesh of fate our heads we thrust.
We can't do what we would, but what we must.
Heredity has got us in a cinch.
(Consoling thought, when you've been on a "bust.")

Hark to the song where spheral voices blend:
"There's no beginning, never will be end."
It makes us nutty; hang the astral chimes!
The table's spread; come, let us dine, my friend.

## THE MEN THAT DON'T FIT IN

THERE'S a race of men that don't fit in,
    A race that can't stay still;
So they break the hearts of kith and kin,
    And they roam the world at will.
They range the field and they rode the flood,
    And they climb the mountain's crest;
Theirs is the curse of the gipsy blood,
    And they don't know how to rest.

    If they just went straight they might go far;
        They are strong and brave and true;
    But they're always tired of the things that are,
        And they want the strange and new.
    They say: "Could I find my proper groove,
        What a deep mark I would make!"
    So they chop and change, and each fresh move
        Is only a fresh mistake.

And each forgets, as he strips and runs,
    With a brilliant, fitful pace,
It's the steady, quiet, plodding ones
    Who win in the lifelong race.
And each forgets that his youth has fled,
    Forgets that his prime is past,
Till he stands one day with a hope that's dead
    In the glare of the truth at last.

    He has failed, he has failed; he has missed his chance;
        He has just done things by half.
    Life's been a jolly good joke on him,
        And now is the time to laugh.
    Ha, ha! He is one of the Legion Lost;
        He was never meant to win;
    He's a rolling stone, and it's bred in the bone;
        He's a man who won't fit in.

## MUSIC IN THE BUSH

O'ER the dark pines she sees the silver moon,
    And in the west, all tremulous, a star;
And soothing sweet she hears the mellow tune
    Of cow-bells jangled in the fields afar.

Quite listless, for her daily stent is done,
    She stands, sad exile, at her rose-wreathed door,
And sends her love eternal with the sun
    That goes to gild the land she'll see no more.

The grave, gaunt pines imprison her sad gaze,
    All still the sky and darkling drearily;
She feels the chilly breath of dear, dead days
    Come sifting through the alders eerily.

  Oh, how the roses riot in their bloom!
    The curtains stir as with an ancient pain;
Her old piano gleams from out the gloom,
    And waits and waits her tender touch in vain.

But now her hands like moonlight brush the keys
    With velvet grace, melodious delight;
And now a sad refrain from overseas
    Goes sobbing on the bosom of the night.

And now she sings. (O singer in the gloom,
    Voicing a sorrow we can ne'er express,
Here in the Farness where we few have room
    Unshamed to show our love and tenderness,

Our hearts will echo, till they beat no more,
    That song of sadness and of motherland;
And stretched in deathless love to England's shore,
    Some day she'll hearken and she'll understand.)

A prima-donna in the shining past,
    But now a mother growing old and grey,
She thinks of how she held a people fast
    In thrall, and gleaned the triumphs of a day.

She sees a sea of faces like a dream;
    She sees herself a queen of song once more;

She sees lips part in rapture, eyes agleam;
    She sings as never once she sang before.

She sings a wild, sweet song that throbs with pain,
    The added pain of life that transcends art,
A song of home, a deep, celestial strain,
    The glorious swan-song of a dying heart.

A lame tramp comes along the railway track,
    A grizzled dog whose day is nearly done:
He passes, pauses, then comes slowly back
    And listens there—an audience of one.

She sings—her golden voice is passion-fraught
    As when she charmed a thousand eager ears;
He listens trembling, and she knows it not,
    And down his hollow cheeks roll bitter tears.

She ceases and is still, as if to pray;
    There is no sound, the stars are all alight—
Only a wretch who stumbles on his way,
    Only a vagrant sobbing in the night.

## THE RHYME OF THE REMITTANCE MAN

THERE'S a four-pronged buck a-swinging in the shadow of my cabin,
   And it roamed the velvet valley till to-day;
But I tracked it by the river, and I trailed it in the cover,
   And I killed it on the mountain miles away.
Now I've had my lazy supper, and the level sun is gleaming
   On the water where the silver salmon play;
And I light my little corn-cob, and I linger softly dreaming,
   In the twilight, of a land that's far away.

Far away, so faint and far, is flaming London, fevered Paris,
   That I fancy I have gained another star;
Far away the din and hurry, far away the sin and worry,
   Far away—God knows they cannot be too far.

Gilded galley-slaves of Mammon—how my purse-proud brothers taunt me!
   I might have been as well-to-do as they
Had I clutched like them my chances, learned their wisdom, crushed my fancies,
   Starved my soul and gone to business every day.

Well, the cherry bends with blossom, and the vivid grass is springing,
   And the star-like lily nestles in the green;
And the frogs their joys are singing, and my heart in tune is ringing,
   And it doesn't matter what I might have been,
While above the scented pine-gloom, piling heights of golden glory,
   The sun-god paints his canvas in the west;
I can couch me deep in clover, I can listen to the story
   Of the lazy, lapping water—it is best.
While the trout leaps in the river, and the blue grouse thrills the cover,
   And the frozen snow betrays the panther's track,
And the robin greets the dayspring with the rapture of a lover,
   I am happy, and I'll nevermore go back.

For I know I'd just be longing for the little old log cabin,
    With the morning-glory clinging to the door,
Till I loathed the city places, cursed the care on all the faces,
    Turned my back on lazar London evermore.

So send me far from Lombard Street, and write me down a failure;
    Put a little in my purse and leave me free.
Say: "He turned from Fortune's offering to follow up a pale lure,
    He is one of us no longer—let him be."
I am one of you no longer: by the trails my feet have broken,
    The dizzy peaks I've scaled, the camp-fire's glow,
By the lonely seas I've sailed in—yea, the final word is spoken,
    I am signed and sealed to nature. Be it so.

## THE LOW-DOWN WHITE

THIS is the pay-day up at the mines, when the bearded brutes come down;
There's money to burn in the streets to-night, so I've sent my klooch to town,
With a haggard face and a ribband of red entwined in her hair of brown.

And I know at the dawn she'll come reeling home with the bottles, one, two, three;
One for herself to drown her shame, and two big bottles for me,
To make me forget the thing I am and the man I used to be.

To make me forget the brand of the dog, as I crouch in this hideous place;
To make me forget once I kindled the light of love in a lady's face,
Where even the squalid Siwash now holds me a black disgrace.

Oh, I have guarded my secret well! And who would dream as I speak
In a tribal tongue like a rogue unhung, 'mid the ranch-house filth and reek,
I could roll to bed with a Latin phrase, and rise with a verse of Greek?

Yet I was a senior prizeman once, and the pride of a college eight;
Called to the bar—my friends were true! but they could not keep me straight;
Then came the divorce, and I went abroad and "died" on the River Plate.

But I'm not dead yet; though with half a lung there isn't time to spare,
And I hope that the year will see me out, and, thank God, no one will care—
Save maybe the little slim Siwash girl with the rose of shame in her hair.

She will come with the dawn, and the dawn is near; I can see its evil glow,
Like a corpse-light seen through a frosty pane in a night of want and woe;
And yonder she comes, by the bleak bull-pines, swift staggering through the snow.

## THE LITTLE OLD LOG CABIN

WHEN a man gits on his uppers in a hard-pan sort of town,
    An' he ain't got nothin' comin', an' he can't afford ter eat,
An' he's in a fix fer lodgin', an' he wanders up an' down,
    An' you'd fancy he'd been boozin', he's so locoed 'bout the feet;
When he's feelin' sneakin' sorry, an' his belt is hangin' slack,
    An' his face is peaked an' grey-like, an' his heart gits down an' whines,
Then he's apt ter git a-thinkin' an' a-wishin' he was back
    In the little ol' log cabin in the shadder of the pines.

When he's on the blazin' desert, an' his canteen's sprung a leak,
    An' he's all alone an' crazy, an' he's crawlin' like a snail,
An' his tongue's so black an' swollen that it hurts him fer to speak,
    An' he gouges down fer water, an' the raven's on his trail;
When he's done with care and cursin', an' he feels more like to cry,
    An' he sees ol' Death a-grinnin', an' he thinks upon his crimes,
Then he's like ter hev' a vision, as he settles down ter die,
    Of the little ol' log cabin an' the roses an' the vines.

Oh, the little ol' log cabin, it's a solemn shinin' mark
    When a feller gits ter sinnin', an' a-goin' ter the wall,
An' folks don't understand him, an' he's gropin' in the dark,
    An' he's sick of bein' cursed at, an' he's longin' fer his call:
When the sun of life's a-sinkin' you can see it 'way above,
    On the hill from out the shadder in a glory 'gin the sky,
An' your mother's voice is callin', an' her arms are stretched in love,
    An' somehow you're glad you're goin', an' you ain't a-scared to die;
When you'll be like a kid again, an' nestle to her breast,
    An' never leave its shelter, an' forget, an' love, an' rest.

## THE YOUNGER SON

IF you leave the gloom of London and you seek a glowing land,
    Where all except the flag is strange and new,
There's a bronzed and stalwart fellow who will grip you by the hand,
    And greet you with a welcome warm and true;
For he's your younger brother, the one you sent away,
    Because there wasn't room for him at home;
And now he's quite contented, and he's glad he didn't stay,
    And he's building Britain's greatness o'er the foam.

When the giant herd is moving at the rising of the sun,
    And the prairie is lit with rose and gold;
And the camp is all a-bustle, and the busy day's begun,
    He leaps into the saddle sure and bold.
Through the round of heat and hurry, through the racket and the rout,
    He rattles at a pace that nothing mars;
And when the night-winds whisper, and camp-fires flicker out,
    He is sleeping like a child beneath the stars.

When the wattle-blooms are drooping in the sombre she-oak glade,
    And the breathless land is lying in a swoon,
He leaves his work a moment, leaning lightly on his spade,
    And he hears the bell-bird chime the Austral noon.
The parakeets are silent in the gum-tree by the creek;
    The ferny grove is sunshine-steeped and still;
But the dew will gem the myrtle in the twilight ere he seek
    His little lonely cabin on the hill.

 Around the purple, vine-clad slope the argent river dreams;
    The roses almost hide the house from view;
A snow-peak of the Winterberg in crimson splendour gleams;
    The shadow deepens down on the karroo.


  He seeks the lily-scented dusk beneath the orange-tree:
    His pipe in silence glows and fades and glows,
And then two little maids come out and climb upon his knee,
    And one is like the lily, one the rose.

He sees his white sheep dapple o'er the green New Zealand plain,
    And where Vancouver's shaggy ramparts frown,
When the sunlight threads the pine-gloom he is fighting might and main
    To clinch the rivets of an Empire down.

  You will find him toiling, toiling, in the south or in the west,
    A child of nature, fearless, frank and free;
And the warmest heart that beats for you is beating in his breast,
    And he sends you loyal greeting o'er the sea.
You've a brother in the Army, you've another in the Church;
    One of you is a diplomatic swell;
You've had the pick of everything and left him in the lurch;
    And yet I think he's doing very well.

I'm sure his life is happy, and he doesn't envy yours;
    I know he loves the land his pluck has won;
And I fancy in the years unborn, while England's fame endures,
    She will come to bless with pride—the Younger Son.

## THE MARCH OF THE DEAD

THE cruel war was over—oh, the triumph was so sweet!
    We watched the troops returning, through our tears;
There was triumph, triumph, triumph down the scarlet glittering street,
    And you scarce could hear the music for the cheers.
And you scarce could see the house-tops for the flags that flew between,
    The bells were pealing madly to the sky;
And every one was shouting for the Soldiers of the Queen,
    And the glory of an age was passing by.

And then there came a shadow, swift and sudden, dark and drear;
    The bells were silent, not an echo stirred.
The flags were drooping sullenly, the men forgot to cheer;
    We waited, and we never spoke a word.
The sky grew darker, darker, till from out the gloomy rack
    There came a voice that checked the heart with dread:
"Tear down, tear down your bunting now, and hang up sable black;
    They are coming—it's the Army of the Dead."

They were coming, they were coming, gaunt and ghastly, sad and slow;
    They were coming, all the crimson wrecks of pride;
With faces seared, and cheeks red smeared, and haunting eyes of woe,
    And clotted holes the khaki couldn't hide.
Oh, the clammy brow of anguish! the livid, foam-flecked lips!
    The reeling ranks of ruin swept along!
The limb that trailed, the hand that failed, the bloody finger-tips!
    And oh, the dreary rhythm of their song!

"They left us on the veldt-side, but we felt we couldn't stop,
    On this, our England's crowning festal day;
We're the men of Magersfontein, we're the men of Spion Kop,
    Colenso,—we're the men who had to pay.
We're the men who paid the blood-price. Shall the grave be all our gain?
    You owe us. Long and heavy is the score.
Then cheer us for our glory now, and cheer us for our pain,
    And cheer us as ye never cheered before."

The folks were white and stricken, and each tongue seemed weighed with lead;
    Each heart was clutched in hollow hand of ice;
And every eye was staring at the horror of the dead,
    The pity of the men who paid the price.
They were come, were come to mock us, in the first flush of our peace;
    Through writhing lips their teeth were all agleam;
They were coming in their thousands—oh, would they never cease!
    I closed my eyes, and then—it was a dream.

There was triumph, triumph, triumph down the scarlet gleaming street;
    The town was mad, a man was like a boy.
A thousand flags were flaming where the sky and city meet;
    A thousand bells were thundering the joy.
There was music, mirth and sunshine; but some eyes shone with regret:
    And while we stun with cheers our homing braves,
O God, in Thy great mercy, let us nevermore forget
    The graves they left behind, the bitter graves.

## "FIGHTING MAC"

## A LIFE TRAGEDY

A PISTOL-SHOT rings round and round the world:
   In pitiful defeat a warrior lies.
A last defiance to dark Death is hurled,
   A last wild challenge shocks the sunlit skies.
   Alone he falls with wide, wan, woeful eyes:
Eyes that could smile at death—could not face shame.

Alone, alone he paced his narrow room,
   In the bright sunshine of that Paris day;
Saw in his thought the awful hand of doom;
   Saw in his dream his glory pass away;
   Tried in his heart, his weary heart, to pray:
"O God! who made me, give me strength to face
The spectre of this bitter, black disgrace."

The burn brawls darkly down the shaggy glen,
   The bee-kissed heather blooms around the door;
He sees himself a barefoot boy again,
   Bending o'er page of legendary lore.
   He hears the pibroch, grips the red claymore,
Runs with the Fiery Cross a clansman true,
Sworn kinsman of Rob Roy and Roderick Dhu.

Eating his heart out with a wild desire,
   One day, behind his counter trim and neat,
He hears a sound that sets his brain afire—
   The Highlanders are marching down the street.
   Oh, how the pipes shrill out, the mad drums beat!
"On to the gates of Hell, my Gordons gay!"
He flings his hated yardstick far away.

He sees the sullen pass, high-crowned with snow,
    Where Afghans cower with eyes of gleaming hate.
He hurls himself against the hidden foe.
      They try to rally—ah, too late, too late!
      Again, defenceless, with fierce eyes that wait
For death, he stands, like baited bull at bay,
And flouts the Boers, that mad Majuba day.

He sees again the murderous Soudan,
    Blood-slaked and rapine swept. He seems to stand
    Upon the gory plain of Omdurman.
      Then Magersfontein, and supreme command
      Over his Highlanders. To shake his hand
A King is proud, and princes call him friend,
And glory crowns his life—and now the end.

The awful end. His eyes are dark with doom;
    He hears the shrapnel shrieking overhead:
He sees the ravaged ranks, the flame-stabbed gloom.
      Oh, to have fallen! the battle-field his bed,
      With Wauchope and his glorious brother-dead.
Why was he saved for this, for this? And now
He raises the revolver to his brow.

In many a Highland home, framed with rude art,
    You'll find his portrait, rough-hewn, stern and square:
It's graven in the Fuyam fellah's heart;
      The Ghurka reads it at his evening prayer;
      The raw lands know it, where the fierce suns glare;
The Dervish fears it. Honour to his name,
Who holds aloft the shield of England's fame.

Mourn for our hero, men of Northern race!
    We do not know his sin; we only know
His sword was keen. He laughed death in the face,
      And struck, for Empire's sake, a giant blow.
      His arm was strong. Ah! well they learnt, the foe.
The echo of his deeds is ringing yet,
Will ring for aye. All else ... let us forget.

## THE WOMAN AND THE ANGEL

AN angel was tired of heaven, as he lounged in the golden street;
His halo was tilted sideways, and his harp lay mute at his feet;
So the Master stooped in His pity, and gave him a pass to go,
For the space of a moon, to the earth-world, to mix with the men below.

He doffed his celestial garments, scarce waiting to lay them straight;
He bade goodbye to Peter, who stood by the golden gate;
The sexless singers of heaven chanted a fond farewell,
And the imps looked up as they pattered on the red-hot flags of hell.

Never was seen such an angel: eyes of a heavenly blue,
Features that shamed Apollo, hair of a golden hue;
The women simply adored him, his lips were like Cupid's bow;
But he never ventured to use them—and so they voted him slow.

Till at last there came One Woman, a marvel of loveliness,
And she whispered to him: "Do you love me?" And he answered that woman, "Yes."
And she said: "Put your arms around me, and kiss me, and hold me—so—"
But fiercely he drew back, saying: "This thing is wrong, and I know."

Then sweetly she mocked his scruples, and softly she him beguiled:
"You, who are verily man among men, speak with the tongue of a child.
We have outlived the old standards; we have burst, like an over-tight thong,
The ancient, outworn, puritanic traditions of Right and Wrong."

Then the Master feared for His angel, and called him again to His side,
For oh, the woman was wondrous, and oh, the angel was tried.
And deep in his hell sang the Devil, and this was the strain of his song:
"The ancient, outworn, puritanic traditions of Right and Wrong."

## THE RHYME OF THE RESTLESS ONES

WE couldn't sit and study for the law;
   The stagnation of a bank we couldn't stand;
For our riot blood was surging, and we didn't need much urging
To excitements and excesses that are banned.
So we took to wine and drink and other things,
   And the devil in us struggled to be free;
Till our friends rose up in wrath, and they pointed out the path,
And they paid our debts and packed us o'er the sea.

Oh, they shook us off and shipped us o'er the foam,
To the larger lands that lure a man to roam;
     And we took the chance they gave
     Of a far and foreign grave,
And we bade goodbye for evermore to home.

And some of us are climbing on the peak,
   And some of us are camping on the plain;
By pine and palm you'll find us, with never claim to bind us,
By track and trail you'll meet us once again.

We are fated serfs to freedom—sky and sea;
   We have failed where slummy cities overflow;
But the stranger ways of earth know our pride and know our worth,
And we go into the dark as fighters go.

Yes, we go into the night as brave men go,
Though our faces they be often streaked with woe;
     Yet we're hard as cats to kill,
     And our hearts are reckless still,
And we've danced with death a dozen times or so.

And you'll find us in Alaska after gold,
   And you'll find us herding cattle in the South.
We like strong drink and fun; and when the race is run,
   We often die with curses in our mouth.

We are wild as colts unbroke, but never mean;
   Of our sins we've shoulders broad to bear the blame;
But we'll never stay in town, and we'll never settle down,
   And we'll never have an object or an aim.

No, there's that in us that time can never tame;
And life will always seem a careless game;
     And they'd better far forget—
     Those who say they love us yet—
Forget, blot out with bitterness our name.

## NEW YEAR'S EVE

IT'S cruel cold on the water-front, silent and dark and drear;
    Only the black tide weltering, only the hissing snow;
And I, alone, like a storm-tossed wreck, on this night of the glad New Year,
    Shuffling along in the icy wind, ghastly and gaunt and slow.

They're playing a tune in McGuffy's saloon, and it's cheery and bright in there
    (God! but I'm weak—since the bitter dawn, and never a bite of food);
I'll just go over and slip inside—I mustn't give way to despair—
    Perhaps I can bum a little booze if the boys are feeling good.

They'll jeer at me, and they'll sneer at me, and they'll call me a whiskey soak;
    ("Have a drink? Well, thankee kindly, sir, I don't mind if I do.")
A drivelling, dirty gin-joint fiend, the butt of the bar-room joke;
    Sunk and sodden and hopeless—"Another? Well, here's to you!"

McGuffy is showing a bunch of the boys how Bob Fitzsimmons hit;
    The barman is talking of Tammany Hall, and why the ward boss got fired;
I'll just sneak into a corner, and they'll let me alone a bit;
    The room is reeling round and round ... O God, but I'm tired, I'm tired....

Roses she wore on her breast that night. Oh, but their scent was sweet;
    Alone we sat on the balcony, and the fan-palms arched above;
The witching strain of a waltz by Strauss came up to our cool retreat,
    And I prisoned her little hand in mine, and I whispered my plea of love.

Then sudden the laughter died on her lips, and lowly she bent her head;
    And oh, there came in the deep, dark eyes a look that was heaven to see
And the moments went, and I waited there, and never a word was said,
    And she plucked from her bosom a rose of red, and shyly gave it to me.

Then the music swelled to a crash of joy, and the lights blazed up like day;
    And I held her fast to my throbbing heart, and I kissed her bonny brow;
"She is mine, she is mine for evermore!" the violins seemed to say,
    And the bells were ringing the New Year in—O God! I can hear them now.

Don't you remember that long, last waltz, with its sobbing, sad refrain?
    Don't you remember that last goodbye, and the dear eyes dim with tears?
Don't you remember that golden dream, with never a hint of pain,
    Of lives that would blend like an angel-song in the bliss of the coming year?

Oh, what have I lost! What have I lost! Ethel, forgive, forgive!
    The red, red rose is faded now, and it's fifty years ago.
'Twere better to die a thousand deaths than live each day as I live!
    I have sinned, I have sunk to the lowest depths—but oh, I have suffered so!

Hark! Oh hark! I can hear the bells!... Look! I can see her there,
    Fair as a dream ... but it fades ... And now—I can hear the dreadful hum
Of the crowded court ... See! the Judge looks down ... NOT GUILTY, my Lord, I swear ...
The bells, I can hear the bells again ... Ethel, I come, I come!...


"Rouse up, old man, it's twelve o'clock. You can't sleep here, you know.
    Say! ain't you got no sentiment? Lift up your muddled head;
Have a drink to the glad New Year, a drop before you go—
    You darned old dirty hobo ... My God! Here, boys! He's DEAD!"

## COMFORT

SAY! You've struck a heap of trouble—
   Bust in business, lost your wife;
No one cares a cent about you,
   You don't care a cent for life;
Hard luck has of hope bereft you,
   Health is failing, wish you'd die—
Why, you've still the sunshine left you,
   And the big, blue sky.

      Sky so blue it makes you wonder
         If it's heaven shining through;
      Earth so smiling 'way out yonder,
         Sun so bright it dazzles you;
      Birds a-singing, flowers a-flinging
         All their fragrance on the breeze;
      Dancing shadows, green, still meadows—
         Don't you mope, you've still got these.

These, and none can take them from you;
These, and none can weigh their worth.

What! you're tired and broke and beaten?—
   Why, you're rich—you've got the earth!
Yes, if you're a tramp in tatters,
   While the blue sky bends above,
You've got nearly all that matters,
   You've got God, and God is love.

## PREMONITION

'TWAS a year ago and the moon was bright
   (Oh, I remember so well, so well),
I walked with my love in a sea of light,
   And the voice of my sweet was a silver bell.

     And sudden the moon grew strangely dull,
       And sudden my love had taken wing;
     I looked on the face of a grinning skull,
       I strained to my heart a ghastly thing.

'Twas but fantasy, for my love lay still
   In my arms with her tender eyes aglow,
And she wondered why my lips were chill,
   Why I was silent and kissed her so.

     A year has gone and the moon is bright,
       A gibbous moon like a ghost of woe;
     I sit by a new-made grave to-night,
       And my heart is broken—it's strange, you know.

## THE TRAMPS

CAN you recall, dear comrade, when we tramped God's land together,
    And we sang the old, old Earth-song, for our youth was very sweet;
When we drank and fought and lusted, as we mocked at tie and tether,
    Along the road to Anywhere, the wide world at our feet.

Along the road to Anywhere, when each day had its story;
    When time was yet our vassal, and life's jest was still unstale;
When peace unfathomed filled our hearts as, bathed in amber glory,
    Along the road to Anywhere we watched the sunsets pale.

Alas! the road to Anywhere is pitfalled with disaster;
    There's hunger, want, and weariness, yet O we loved it so!
As on we tramped exultantly, and no man was our master,
    And no man guessed what dreams were ours, as swinging heel and toe,
We tramped the road to Anywhere, the magic road to Anywhere,
    The tragic road to Anywhere, such dear, dim years ago.

## L'ENVOI

YOU who have lived in the Land,
    You who have trusted the trail;
You who are strong to withstand,
    You who are swift to assail;
Songs have I sung to beguile,
    Vintage of desperate years
Hard as a harlot's smile,
    Bitter as unshed tears.

        Little of joy or mirth,
            Little of ease I sing;
        Sagas of men of earth,
            Humanly suffering,
        Such as you all have done;
            Savagely faring forth,
        Sons of the midnight sun,
            Argonauts of the North.

Far in the land God forgot
    Glimmers the lure of your trail;
Still in your lust are you taught
    Even to win is to fail.
Still must you follow and fight
    Under the vampire wing;
There in the long, long night
    Hoping and vanquishing.

        Husbandmen of the Wild,
            Reaping a barren gain;
        Scourged by desire, reconciled
            Unto disaster and pain;
        These my songs are for you,
            You who are seared with the brand:
        God knows I have tried to be true;
            Please God you will understand.

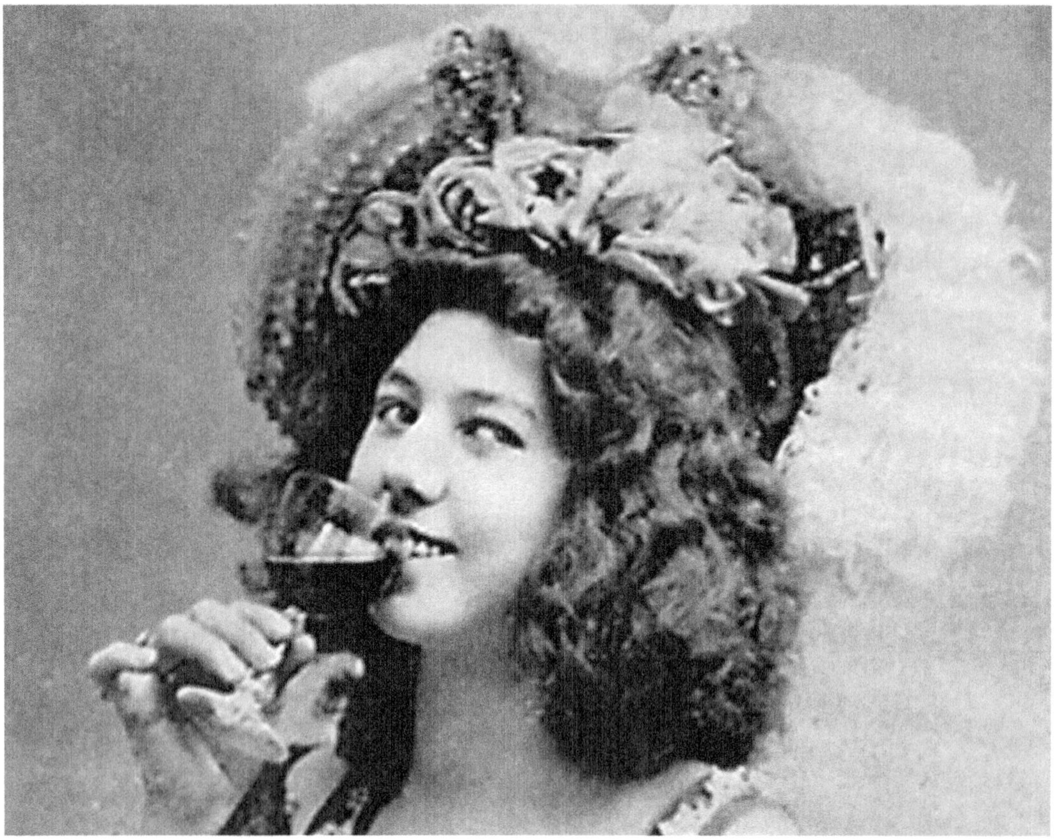